Don't STAY IN YOUR *Grief*

by
Lacey Whittaker *&* Mary Ackerman

Edited by Lil Barcaski
Published by: GWN Publishing

www.GWNPublishing.com

Cover Design: Kristina Conatser
Captured by KC Design

ISBN: 979-8-9863922-7-1

Dedication:

To all who are suffering grief and
loss.

Introduction:

GRIEF. In this world we will see it. We will walk in it. We will endure it. In this lifetime on earth, grief will be a part of our course. Distress, deep sorrow, and pain. Suffering. We have a God that wants to be there, hold our hand, and see us through. We have a God. Will you let Him help you?

In this book are prayers, poems, and testimonies from people that have experienced deep grief and struggle. I hope these words help heal your grieving souls.

Jesus is the only answer and release.

"All praises belong to the God and Father of our Lord Jesus Christ. For he is the Father of tender mercy and the God of endless comfort."

2 CORINTHIANS 1:3 TPT

The God of comfort and compassion. The God that cares. Feel the pain. He knows the pain. He sees the pain. Don't suppress but express the honest, raw heart full of hurt and pain. Even Jesus cried out to the Father in the garden of Gethsemane. Please, I don't want this. Let this pass from me. You are in good company in your grief.

Perfection. Flawless. Excellent. Ideal.
Why do I struggle when I know it's not
real? We can strive our whole lives and
never reach perfection. Perfection is
Jesus. Maybe that's why I long to live for
perfection. All it does is kill and destroy.
It makes me crazy. It makes my loved
ones want to run, I'm sure.

Perfection is disgrace. Our bodies will
never be perfect no matter how hard we
try. Our children will never be perfect as
much as we would love to portray, pray,
strive.

Perfection is only You, Jesus. Our
marriages will never be perfect. It takes
hard work, communication, forgiveness,
and love.

Help me see this in a new way. Help
me live to want to please You, knowing
sometimes I will lose. Help me to see that
perfect is just an ideal. Help me get past
the way I feel. Help me be flawed and ok.
Help me see. Please, oh please, perfection
leave me.

The punches kept coming, one after another and another. We found ourselves sitting in that hospital room with our ten-year-old baby girl. Her face was sunken in, she was gray, scared, dehydrated, and skinny as a rail. So helpless, laying there.

As the doctor walked in with the news, we wondered if he was an angel. He was so gentle, here to soften the blow of the news that was going to change our lives as we knew it. Then he said, "your daughter has Type 1 Diabetes." We just sat there and cried.

If I could've taken this from her, I would've. I cried out to God please take this from her and give to me. We watched the countless finger pricks, the abundance of shots. We soon realized that this was going to be our new normal.

As we took our girl home, the worry, panic, and anxiety set in. Would she make it through the night? How was she going to be able to go to school. What if?

What if something happens? What if? I couldn't control this. I couldn't control this if I tried. What if this consumed me all my day and nights. As I look back, only the Lord could've got us through those four months of hell.

My mind still wonders from time to time, and I freak out. When the panic comes on, I remember to pray and take a deep breath of trust and faith. My daughter is His. He has her. He will protect her. He loves her. He knows. I trust her with Him; this I know.

"Jesus wept."

JOHN 11:35 NKJV

Love everlasting. Love is everlasting, love is strong. Our love for you, son, will always be, even though you are now gone. Mom and dad miss you, son, so very much. We can no longer put our arms around you, son. To love and feel your special touch.

Son, if you could only see all the special friends you left behind. Son, to your father and I, they have been so very kind. To them, I know, you will always be remembered in their mind.

My prayer, to all the moms and dads, show that special daughter or son all your love and care, for tomorrow is not promised and you may awake and find he or she not there.

Teach your children, life is short. Love is forever, God's love is the only way. If we can live to show our love, we can all be together again someday.

So someday, son, when our work is through, God will call us home, forever, to be with you. There, our love will all be renewed.

Love and miss you forever,

Mom.

— *Mary Ackerman* —

"Yahweh is my best friend and my shepherd. I always have more than enough. He offers a resting place for me in His luxurious love. His tracks take me to an oasis of peace near the quiet brook of bliss. That's where He restores and revives my life. He opens before me the right path and leads me along in his footsteps of righteousness so that I can bring honor to His name. Even when your path takes me through the valley of deepest darkness, fear will never conquer me, for You already have! Your authority is my strength and my peace. The comfort of Your love takes away my fear. I'll never be lonely, for You are near. You become my delicious feast even when my enemies dare to fight. You anoint me with the

fragrance of Your Holy Spirit;
You give me all I can drink of
You until my cup overflows. So,
why would I fear the future?
Only goodness and tender love
pursue me all the days of my
life. Then afterward, when my
life is through, I'll return to
Your glorious presence to be
forever with You!"

PSALMS 23:1-6 TPT

The loss of friendships cut deep. It's a deep grief, a deep pain. It's different. That friend was my one. The one I never thought would not be the one. I never thought we would grow apart. Never. When I lost her in that season, I was lonely. I felt really left out. She was still going, and I was changing. I felt the Lord moving me in His direction, not staying stagnant, but moving. I would love to say, once I realized this, I was good, but I wasn't, and I still miss her after all these years. With that said, I wouldn't trade where He has taken me, for all the past, as I know, I'm where I need to be at last. He has given me new friends to share and love. with this, I hold dear. I cherish them. I will never forget that one friend I had, even until the very end.

If I wanted peace, I had to look to the King of Kings. If I wanted peace, I knew I had to stay there. If I truly wanted peace through grief, I had to pray He stayed there with me. I prayed. I looked to Him. I prayed for strength. I prayed for peace. I didn't know another way. I prayed He would give me peace. I prayed and woke up. I prayed. I chose to give Him everything. I chose to walk with Him. I had to choose, and with that, I had peace to get me through.

Shattered heart. My heart is broken in pieces. Shattered. How do I pick up and begin again? How do I live with you gone? My heart beats differently now. It's so different with you gone. Why did you have to leave me? Why couldn't I go first? How do I live without you? I'm so lonely and sad. Will my heart ever feel again? Will it ever really heal with you gone? It's shattered. A shattered heart. Lord, I'm asking you to heal this broken, ever-loving heart.

Guilt is hard. Mom guilt is harder. Why did I stay? Why did I let him treat my kids that way? Why, oh why, only He knows. Why couldn't I let go? Why, oh why, did it take me so long? Why did it take me to knocking down the door to see my child trying to commit suicide? Why, oh why, I ask these things? Why, oh why, Lord help me find a way. Thank you for saving her that day.

I walked away and never looked back. It took me a few times, but I walked away. Why did I walk away? Why did I walk away from that life, I knew so well? Why, oh why, is the story I shall tell. I was no longer going to walk that way. I lived my life enabling, putting You and myself last. I was all about my husband and children, right or wrong, I never made the time for You, Lord. I was trying to get by in this barking world. I was trying to love my kids by the to-dos. I was a wife that never said no. I was a mother that always enabled, even when I knew to stop. I was that woman that got beat down just to get back up again. Got beat down and never would truly win, until that day I found You, Lord. I found You on the floor. Until that day I found You, Lord, something changed. I found my roar; I found my voice to speak up, to speak truth. Lord, I walked away from that life because I chose You.

Everyone experiences grief in some way and there are diffcrent types of grief.

I became familiar with both experiencing and witnessing deep grief at a very young age. I grieved for my mother being in an abusive relationship with my father who never abused his children and who I admired and loved. I grieved the loss of my brother when he died in a car accident and, along with my own grief, I was a witness to my parents' grieving the loss of their child, which was much worse. I grieved the loss of their marriage and the life I had known when their grief, combined, was too much to live in and they divorced. I grieved the loss of relationships and friendships.

I grieved the loss of my mother. When a daughter loses her mother, it's a special kind of grief. We are literally part of our mothers. We are grown inside of them. Being separated physically through their death is a very lonely grief, but also a very spiritual one. We are still connected to our mothers when they go home to heaven, and while the loneliness here on earth can feel overwhelming, we feel a little more connected to heaven because they are there, and a little more connected to Jesus because our mothers are with Him.

I grieved the loss of myself when I was in an abusive relationship. I became an empty shell of only grief and sadness and I now know the only thing giving me strength was the Grace of God.

I grieved the loss of my grandmother. Many people know this grief. I don't know how to explain it, other than to say that this is a softer grief that is steeped in pleasant memories. They become our ancestors who we tell stories about and whose recipes we keep in special places. Their things become precious mementos of their time with us.

I grieved the loss of my daughters' innocence at the hands of a man I trusted. This was the deepest, most excruciatingly painful grief I had ever experienced. This kind of grief was different than all the rest. This grief felt like it could drown me or smother me. It felt like no matter how hard I cried and how much I screamed, I could not get this grief, this strangling weight, out of my chest. I couldn't breathe. I couldn't think. I was filled with rage one moment and completely unable to move with sadness the next. I was strong, and protective, and ready to fight for my daughter, and at the same time I was so full of fear, and anxiety, and hopelessness, and GUILT. The guilt and the disappointment in myself were always there. I felt I couldn't trust myself or anyone else ever again.

But that wasn't the worst part. The worst part was witnessing with clear eyes, my daughter's trauma and her own grief. It was almost unbearable. But you know what is really miraculous about the kind of grief that brings you all the way down to the ground and strips you of any way to stuff it down or ignore it or push it aside?

You realize that you can't do it by yourself. God is the only one who can. He is the only one that can take your guilt, your shame, your deep grief and wash it away. He is the only one that can set you free from that. And when He does, you **KNOW** it's Him because you **KNOW** in that kind of grief that you don't have that strength. God used grief to shape me, and ultimately grief took me straight to Jesus's feet.

I didn't grow up in church, I didn't have a relationship with Jesus. I believed in God, but I wasn't saved until I experienced the one thing that I knew could not have been from my own strength and power but had to be of God, and that is when I was delivered from grief.

— *Kasey Carroll* —

What are some keys to handle grief? Don't blame or shame yourself. Give them to Jesus. Know they are in the loving arms of Jesus. That's our hope. Letting them go. Know the Lord has plans for you to continue here. Go through, and don't get stuck in your grieving. Call on Jesus. He hears your every cry. Be thankful to Jesus for loving them and knowing His plan is always the best plan even though we may never understand. He sees the whole picture when we may only see in a tunnel at the time of overwhelming grief.

Why did you have to leave? In a sudden moment. I didn't know that was going to be the last time I heard, "I love her with all my heart." I didn't know that was going to be the last. I would ask you back in a second if you were healthy and not sick. I would ask you back, but I know the Father has you. He knows when it's our time to go. I cherish all those memories. I hold on with the support of our family and friends. I hold on by a song. I pray, Lord, give me strength. I lose my faith and get it back. Most days I cry, and that helps with the healing. I still can't believe you are really gone. It seems like a whirlwind since that day six months ago. Please God help me move along.

I've never felt so alone, and I've never felt so loved in the same moment. When everyone leaves your side. When you are left alone to cry. When no one is there to check on you. When you sit and feel you only lose. When your children don't even call to say hey, I was thinking of you today. When your parents are gone, and you are the only one. When you feel pain from those yesterdays. I've never felt so alone but so loved. Jesus, You are the only one. You are the only one. You are truly the only one. You love so deep, so true, you never leave me apart from You. Thank you for loving me like You do. Thank you for seeing me on these lonely days, I need You.

It's almost been a year since I have seen your face. It's almost been a year and you feel further away. It's almost been a year and, each day, I wake up missing you, longing to hear you say, dad I'm ready to go. I'm ready for this. Oh, how I long to hug you again. Oh, how I long to touch you and see you grow. Oh, how I long. How am I supposed to go on without you here? I don't understand. There are so many fears. How am I supposed to go on? Why did this happen to you? It's not fair. I just want to die with you. I want to be with you again. Help me, I'm crying out, help me to live again. Help me, please help me move along and learn how to live with you gone. Please help me, I can't even seem to breathe. Help me see better days. Help me Father, help me stay.

The absence of your presence. I know the absence of your presence even though I feel you, oh so near. I touch you in spirit with God's love. To hear your laughter, to see your face, to feel your love from above. I look into the clouds sometimes of this wondrous, large, blue sky. I see the outline of your face and it brings a tear to my eye. I feel God chose you for some special chore. He said, come home with Me son to live in peace forevermore. Today is forever until tomorrow comes. I'll feel the absence of your presence, son, until we're all called home, when our Lord and master says, well done.

— *Mary Ackerman* —

"He will wipe away every tear from their eyes and eliminate death entirely. No one will mourn or weep any longer. The pain of wounds will no longer exist, for the old order has ceased."

REVELATION 21:4 TPT

One day. We have hope for one day. One day. Even when you don't see how you can make it another day. One day. He promised one day. One day. One day. He will take this away. One day. One day. One day we will live a new day. One day. We will sing great praise. One day. We will see our loved ones again. One day. It's our hope. One day death will be wiped away. One day.

I cried out that day I lost you. I cried out until I couldn't cry anymore. I cried out that day. I cried out that day I lost you. I cried out that day. I cried out that day. I cried. I cried knowing the Lord was the only one that was going to see me through this kind of pain. I cried out that day. I still cry. I cry now in another way.

When I lost my father, the world went quiet. I remember being on my way home, in the back seat scrolling through my phone, waiting to get home to see my dad, even though I knew it would be the last time.

I received a text 30 minutes before arriving, from a family member telling me they were sorry for my loss before I even knew he was gone. As I got out of the car, everyone looked at me with sadness and no words. I walked inside and went straight to my dad. He was gone but I held him for a while. He was cold and small. I don't remember much else about that day.

No one knows, but after it happened— for years—I didn't run to God, I yelled at Him. I told Him how unfair He was being, that there was no reason for this loss other than His selfishness to not care enough to take care of my father.

I went to the lake and, while sobbing and screaming, promised I would be and do anything if He would let him appear in front of me one more time, "**JUST BRING HIM BACK**," I screamed. I felt alone when no one came.

I held that grudge against God for years. I rebelled, became dependent on the wrong things and the wrong people because the right ones made me remember. Even when my father visited me in my dreams, there was no thanks to Him for the comfort, just more anger for my loss.

I've carried guilt with my grief. The guilt of not being there for him more, since I was living in a different state at the time. The guilt of all I had done as a child/preteen/young adult to selfishly to have my way without consequence.

Throughout the eight years that my dad has been gone I have hated God, lost faith in God, questioned God, and then more recently felt unworthy of Him, but not once did I try to get closer to Him or thank Him.

I never thanked Him for the father that I did have that so many don't. The one who I would dance in front of after he got home from work just to be annoying while he was watching TV. The one who took me fishing for the first time outside our house when I was little. The one who tried to teach me to shoot a gun I could barely hold when it kicked back. The one who taught me how to golf. The one who would light up the day by surprising me at a volleyball or basketball game. The one who celebrated my first job at McDonald's and bragged about me. The one who taught me as much as I would be patient for learning about with cars. The man that found out I was pregnant and terrified at 18 and walked into my room just to tell me he loved me anyway.

A man of few words, full of love for me. A man who did just as much for others as he did for me. God blessed me with the best without praise or appreciation from me.

Grief is hard, and I don't believe it ever leaves you while you're still here. I am lucky enough to have a family who loves God. A family that is helping me find my way back to Him. Even though I have a long way to go, my grief is more bearable.

My walk with God is in progress, and I'm rebuilding my relationship with Him slowly and releasing my guilt. That's the beautiful thing about God, and the hardest thing to understand, no matter how long we go without praising Him, you'll always be welcomed home with Him.

I believe God doesn't always need us to run to Him, just start going in His direction and you'll find your way.

Just like I'm finding mine.

— *Chelsea Shiner* —

The emptiness. The void. The hollow, barren space. It's deep. What once was filled is no longer here. It's empty. I feel so empty. How can one feel so empty? I long for that feeling I had. It's gone. I lost you. I lost a part of me. I'm so empty I can barely breathe. Lord, I'm crying out, please fill me. Please help me.

What kind of man that you trusted takes the innocence of your daughter? What kind of man does this?

Where did I go wrong? I'm full of guilt and disappoint. How did I not see this? How did I not protect my daughter? How? Why? How? Why?

I've felt deep grief, but I've never felt this type. My daughter. The deepest, most excruciatingly painful grief. It drowns and smothers me. I can't breathe. How do I go on from here with all this sadness, rage and fear? How do I? It's more than I can bear witnessing my daughter's trauma from this horrible act of evil. It's almost more than I can bear.

The miraculous thing about grief is when you meet Jesus at His feet. I could not do this alone. I needed God. I needed Him to give me strength and I needed Him to take this guilt and shame. I needed Him to wash it away. He did that day. He did.

He set me free. I will forever be indebted for this victory.

"But may the God of all grace, who called us to His eternal glory by Christ Jesus, after you have suffered a while, perfect, establish, strengthen, and settle you."

I PETER 5:10 NKJV

God gives us strength in our suffering if we call upon His name. Cry out to Him. Take His hand. Let Him lead. Let Him heal. Let Him be. Suffering won't last forever. His grace will prevail.

Do you want to get even? Are you so angry you can't see? Are you wanting to get even? The one that took my son. My son is now gone. I don't know how to move on. My son is gone. I want to get even. I want to repay. I want to take what was taken from me.

I want to get even. I know it's wrong, but it would feel so good to get even. I want to get even. I want to sin. I want to take the life that took my son away. I want to get even, I say. I know it's wrong, Lord. I know it's wrong, but what do I do?

I want to get even, though I know I still will lose. Help me Lord, help me release this pain. Help me Lord, forgive and see brighter days. I'm fighting to stay alive; I'm fighting to live again. Help me Father, I repent of this.

We love and miss you still today. For in our hearts, you will always stay.

But I hold close in my heart.

We are really not that far apart.

I know I will see you again someday.

Until then I wait, watch, and pray.

God has a plan that we don't know, until that day, I'll keep loving you so.

— *Mary Ackerman* —

After losing someone, every day is a new day. A new day of grief and pain. A new day of memories and take away. Every day is a new day. How do I go on? How do I live now with this hurt and pain? How?

Every day is a new day. It starts and ends with one name, Jesus. When all I could say was Jesus, it helped me through. Jesus, Jesus, Jesus. It's the only way. One way. Jesus, the name above all names. Jesus saves our crushed spirits. He saves us. Jesus, it's only Your name I shall say.

It's been a year you have been gone. It's been a year, and I'm here left alone. Raising our children as a single mother is hard. Raising them to live in the light and not the dark.

I'm overwhelmed with stress and anxiety. I'm overwhelmed to the point I simply cannot breathe. I'm overwhelmed with all the firsts we had to see, without you here holding me. I'm overwhelmed, but still trust God. I'm overwhelmed, trying to move on. I'm overwhelmed, but the damage has been done. I'm overwhelmed, help me please be strong. I'm overwhelmed, but ready to live again. I'm overwhelmed, fighting to feel again. I'm overwhelmed, but I know this feeling won't last forever, that's my hope as I endeavor.

Ease this broken heart inside me, I plead. Ease, please ease, this pain and suffering. Ease. Please ease. I can't feel because it hurts so bad. Please ease this heart. Will it ever be glad? Please ease, show me You can. Ease this heart Lord, it's all I have.

I give this to You. I give it to You. What else can I do? I give this to You. I give it to You. Please make me new. Please help me through. I give to You. I have tried again and again. I have sunk into a deeper pit. I give this to You. Lord, have it. I want to start living again. I want to start seeing Your plan. Take this Lord. Take my hand.

When I lost you that day, I chose to consume myself in the Lord. That's the only way. It was the only way I could live without you here. It was never a question. I consumed myself on that day. That was my hope, my trust, my faith. Thank God I knew. Thank God, He sees me though. The loss in my heart is so deep. A part of me will be gone forever. The only cure to this crushed heart is the consumption of the One that made us all. The only cure is to be consumed by the One, our Father that loves.

He's always there. It's spring, and the trees are all budded out. The birds are singing and the grass is starting to grow green. Deep inside, there's a warm feeling because he's always there.

The world goes on, even though his life ended there. It seemed so soon, so unfair. But his love lives forever, you better beware, because he's always there. Hear my message and take it to heart, because even though he's not here, we're not far apart.

— *Mary Ackerman* —

Empty me of me. Empty me of pity and defeat. Fill me with prayer and thanksgiving. Empty me, I ask. Empty me, I am in choosing to live in lack. Empty me, fill me with your goodness and belief. Empty me, free me from me. Empty me, Father, until it's only You I seek.

I didn't know that was going to be the last time. I didn't know as I pulled out of that drive. I felt a nudge to go back in and kiss your face. I'm glad I did, because I didn't know that was going to be the last. I didn't know this was the end, I didn't know.

I'm thankful for Jesus who never left me alone. He gave me comfort all my days. He gave me strength to see another day. He gave me peace knowing we will be together again one day. He gave me you, and now I give you back, not asking why, but knowing the sin of this world takes, not God, is my faith.

The past triggers and I become angry. I become so angry with all the abuse I endured. All the control, the guilt, the lost time. I thought he would change, so I stayed, and I buried it deep in my gut. So helpless and nowhere to turn. I buried it. I held on. I held on so tight thinking one day things would be right. It only left me angry with unforgiveness all these years. Lord, please show me how to forgive and heal.

"The Lord is near to the
heartbroken And He saves
those who are crushed in spirit
(contrite in heart, truly sorry
for their sin)."

PSALMS 34:18 AMP

What does this mean some may ask? I am
the one that lost. I am the one grieving.
I am the one. How am I to repent? They
were taken away from me. I lost my job.
I am still sick after I prayed for healing.

My ten-year dream is no longer a dream,
but a bust. I am the one hurt. In times
of grief, anger, obsession, guilt, and stress
this could be embedded in your heart
making it hard.

Years of placing blame and unforgiveness
could leave you in a pit. That's why we

repent. He wants to save us. Repent that pain and sin today.

Treasured memories. I think of all the times we spent together. Some were good, some were bad, but we made the best of all of them no matter which we had. These are treasured memories I now have. I watched you grow from a little boy into a young man full of life, joy, and hopes for the future. Yes, you had big plans, but these are treasured memories now. It's hard to understand, this is your senior year, son, and you would be graduating with your class, but instead I have your ring to hold and all the treasured memories from the past. You have graduated to a higher class, I pray, that special angel came to get you on that day. These are treasured memories forever in our hearts to stay.

— *Mary Ackerman* —

*"Your eyes saw me when I was
still an unborn child. Every day
of my life was recorded in your
book before one of them had
taken place."*

PSALMS 139:16 GW

When I lost you that day. When I lost
you that day. When I lost you all these
thoughts ran through. All these thoughts
of how I could lose you? What could've
been done differently? How could I have
changed this so you would still be here
with me? How? All this rage inside of me,
how could this truly be? Then I read. I
read. God numbers our days. I read. The
only thing that helps me through, really
this could not be any different.

Help me let go of the last little bit... I thought I let go but it comes back with another hit. Help me let go of the last little bit. I hear Him say, breathe and release, breathe and release, this you shall reap. A life full of peace. Breathe and release, breathe and release the suffering, the hurt, the pain, release it all now. Be free now, totally set free.

"*Charm is deceitful and beauty is passing, but a woman who fears the Lord, she shall be praised.*"

PROVERBS 31:30 NKJV

What about the grief of body image? That grief runs deep in me. I can hate on myself for every little thing. I can pick myself apart in no time, it's true. It's sad, and a sick game I play. I play with ideals, comparison, defeat.

Oh, I play, and I reap. I reap jealousy and insecurity. I reap self-doubt and more lies. I reap the evil and sin I have chosen to walk in. When is enough, enough? When do look up and look to God? I have set my mind on things and ideals of this world.

Today, I say, no more. He has chosen and created me. I shall start thinking of all these things. Lord, fix my focus on above and not all these images that I hate to love.

Help me God, I repent. I am sorry for going against this body You have given. I'm sorry Lord, I repent. I choose to focus on being heaven sent.

"He has made everything beautiful and appropriate in its time. He has also planted eternity [a sense of divine purpose] in the human heart [a mysterious longing which nothing under the sun can satisfy, except God]—yet man cannot find out (comprehend, grasp) what God has done (His overall plan) from the beginning to the end."

ECCLESIASTES 3:11 AMP

The betraying friend. The friend that just went away in a day. She didn't say goodbye, she didn't say anything. She left, and I never talked to her again. She left because she realized we were so different. She couldn't go any further, so she stopped. She left, and for months my heart dropped.

It was so hurt, lost, and confused. I couldn't figure out how I lost and hurt so bad. I couldn't remember when I last felt this bad. It hurt, and took a year to move on. Now that I have, I feel so strong. Sometimes you need a Judas to show you. I'm glad you did, for I learned a lot from you.

"A father of the fatherless, a defender of widows, Is God in His holy habitation."

PSALMS 68:5 NKJV

The child left on the doorstep of the hospital room. The widow left by her husband's death bed. The loss. The pain. The wondering why and will things ever be the same.

The abandonment from your mother and father. The shame that follows you sometimes to your grave. How could they give up their child without a story to tell? The widow that is now left alone in her home.

God looks on. He looks on. He looks on. He has called us to love and serve. Don't forget these things He has called us to do. Don't forget we are to love them through.

"Pure and undefiled religion before God and the Father is this: to visit orphans and widows in their trouble, and to keep oneself unspotted from the world."

JAMES 1:27 NKJV

I remember being pregnant and felt something go wrong. I felt it deep within. I felt like coming out of my skin. My baby growing inside of me. How God, could I lose? How could I lose this baby?

The D&C felt so wrong. Why was I allowing this done even knowing my baby was well gone? This loss felt like no other. As a mother felt like no other.

I fell into a deep depression and shame. I fell for months, and remained the same. I fell, but that day, I chose to pray and not be mad. That day, I chose peace. That day, I chose to allow God to help me through this pain. That day, I changed.

*"Don't be obsessed with money
but live content with what
you have, for you always have
God's presence. For hasn't He
promised you, "I will never
leave you, never! And I will not
loosen my grip on your life!"*

HEBREWS 13:5 TPT

What about when you lose your money,
your job, your dream, your retirement?
What about the loss of the security you
had? What about the loss that you see
and must live with? What about when
those things are sold just to not lose your
home? What about that loss? We have a
God that sees. We have a God that wants
to be your one. Your provider. Your one.
We have a God. Hold on. Surrender to
Him. We have a God that loves to see
us win.

Divorce. Separate. Divide. Part ways.
How does this make sense when you are a
God of love, peace, forgiveness, all these
things you teach? Reconciliation. How
does this make sense? How does this
make sense when I prayed time and time
and time again? I always prayed we would
win, we would overcome. How does this
make sense? I don't understand how this
is part of my plan. Divorce such a harsh
word. We've struggled, we have let go.
Help me see this as You see this, Lord.
Help me be brave and choose. Help me,
I am asking You. Help me Lord, I need
You every step of the way. Help me Lord,
I'm crying out. Help me Lord, You are all
I'm about. I know I can walk through this
battle with Your shining truth. I know I
can walk because I have You.

I heard that phone ring. My doctors name popped up and my heart sank. I answered and heard the news I never wanted to hear. You have cancer, I am sorry dear. The next moments I couldn't breathe. Would I live to see my family? All those fears and why's came flooding out.

If I'm honest, I had some doubt. Why God? Why me? I have a little girl, can't you see. I can't do this, pick someone else. I can't do this, please help take it away like I know You can. Take it away, please, I want to see better days.

The next six months we're a blur. All I held onto was one powerful word. Jesus. Jesus is all I could say. Jesus, help me through to see another day. Jesus, take this anxiety and panic attacks. Jesus, take them, I can't see past. Jesus, take care of my little girl. Jesus, heal me so I can live forevermore.

As I look back, I am thankful for that pain because I'm brand new by calling on His name. I am thankful for that pain, for I have learned to live life in a new way.

Can you still feel blessed when you are distressed? Can you delight when things are not alright? Can you find joy when you are walking in deep sorrow? Can you cheer when you feel fear? Can you exalt His name when you feel so much pain? You can. You can when you choose Him. When you say, no matter what I choose You, Lord. I choose You to see me through this. I will choose You every time. Help me, Lord, choose You in the hard days. Help me choose to praise Your name. Help me today. I choose You, Lord, to stay.

Angry and stressed. Feeling guilty and obsessed? Grief brings all these things. They come on thick and send you into a deep dark pit if you allow them to; if you don't call on the name of Jesus to help you through. All these things come in a thought and how you choose to speak. Jesus, please come help me. I'm tired of choosing angry instead of peace. I'm tired of placing blame instead of asking for Your eyes to see. Lord, I'm tired and I am full of guilt and shame. I'm tired of obsessing in the worst ways. I'm tired, Lord, come today. I'm tired, please help me in a new way. Help me to see with Your eyes of grace. Help me live by faith.

Grief when you don't release. Grief. The frustration, annoyance, and the long suffering of grief. It wreaks havoc inside me, sometimes crippling. The grief torments and stays when you don't open the door to let it out. Don't let the grief stay one more day. For years, grief has built up inside of me. A trigger I didn't see, opening new wounds where I couldn't stand to breathe. Breathe in peace, let the rest go. Breathe in peace, let the rest go. Be set free from the internal suffering. Be set free.

What kind of legacy are you leaving? Are you stuck? Are you ready to give up? Is the fight gone because it's been way too long? What kind of legacy will you leave? When times get tough, do you stay in anger, bitter, grief? There is a savior that died to set us free from any battle we face. Look to Him today. See with eyes of faith. He will rescue us when we call on His name.

The fruits that produce after that trial. The battle that almost took you out. The fruits that produce after that hardship. The fruits that produce when you are tossed and thrown. Oh, the fruits that produce. The character built. See the character after the pruning and plucking. See it. The fruits produced.

"and endurance, proven character (spiritual maturity); and proven character, hope and confident assurance [of eternal salvation]."

ROMANS 5:4 AMP

Losing my dad. I felt so sad. I felt so lost. I felt so empty. I know you battled long. You were sick, you were done. You had the faith. You kept a smile on your face. When you left, you took a piece of me with you. You were my go-to. You were my dad, my boss, my guy that had all the answers. I know you are healed and whole. I know you are in heaven and that's my hope. Until that day I see your face, I will pray and seek the One that died to save. Because He did, I know I will be ok, I will see you again someday.

I still find myself missing you. I still find myself reaching for you. I still find myself loving. After eight years, I still find myself wondering. I miss you every day. I long to see your face. Eternity is only a step away. My faith is to see you in heaven one day. That's what I hold on to. I thank God you are there. I thank God, He cares. I thank God my broken heart has mended. I thank God. I look back on that day you left. Those nights, those weeks. I felt my heart break like never before. I felt it fall on the floor. I was empty. I felt like I was having a heart attack. My heart hurt so bad. It ached. I miss you. I am looking forward to that one sweet, holy day. Thank you, Lord, for carrying me through. Thank you Lord, I need you.

"He heals the wounds of every shattered heart."

PSALMS 147:3 TPT

Acknowledgements:

Kasey Carroll, Chelsea Shiner, Mike Cornman, Nellie Machelett, Lindsey Machelett, Rita Krone, Brenda Shiner and Bill Ackerman.

In precious memory of Jake Ackerman, Stanley Shiner, Gavin Cornman, and Bill Machelett. You are all loved and missed dearly.

About the authors:

Mary Ackerman resides in Sullivan, MO. She was saved and baptized at 11-years-old. She has always tried to live and walk faithfully with the Lord. She's loves walking into the house of the Lord and enjoys making the churches beautiful with her love for decor. Her heart is to reach the lost and to be that shining light to them.

Lacey Whittaker is the Founder of True Love Ministries. She loves to write. Her heart is for everyone to know that the most important relationship you can have is the one on one with our Father. She resides in Bourbon, MO.

God's Love
To End All

His **G**-Grace
Mercy **R**-Revealed
Heals **I**- Internal
To **E**-Embrace
Total **F**-Freedom & Release

brings Peace
and Joy